# ACHIEVING EXCELLENCE

*— So Good —*

## ROBERT HELLER

D0063803

DK

DK PUBLISHING, INC.

## A DK PUBLISHING BOOK

### www.dk.com

Produced for Dorling Kindersley
by Cooling Brown

**Editor** Amanda Lebentz
**Designer** Elly King
**Creative Director** Arthur Brown

**DTP Designer** Jason Little
**Production Controller** Silvia La Greca

**Series Editor** Adèle Hayward
**Series Art Editor** Tassy King
**US Editors** Gary Werner, Chuck Wills
**Managing Editors** Stephanie Jackson, Jonathan Metcalf
**Managing Art Editor** Nigel Duffield

First American Edition, 1999
10 9 8 7 6 5 4 3 2 1

Published in the United States by
DK Publishing, Inc.
95 Madison Avenue, New York, New York 10016

Library of Congress Cataloging-in-Publication Data

Heller, Robert, 1932-
    Achieving Excellence / by Robert Heller -- 1st American ed.
    p.   cm. -- (Essential managers)
    Includes index.
    ISBN 0-7894-4862-9 (alk.paper)
    1. Management. 2. Self-actualization (Psychology).
3. Success in business 4. Self-realization. I. Title. II. Series.
HD31.H4445 1999
650.1--dc21                                          99-15781
                                                          CIP

Reproduced by Colourscan, Singapore
Printed and bound in Italy by Graphicom srl

# CONTENTS

# ACHIEVING SUCCESS

## BECOMING MORE EFFECTIVE

# INTRODUCTION

Excellence in today's highly competitive workplace demands more than a thorough knowledge of your specialist field. People skills – such as the ability to inspire others, foster a sense of cooperation, and delegate effectively – are of critical importance. Equally vital is the mastery of a range of practical skills – from effective communicating to time management – and a confident, determined attitude toward your career. A balanced mix of all these elements is what differentiates a competent manager from an outstanding one. Achieving Excellence provides you with a comprehensive grounding in all these areas. The practical advice is supplemented by 101 indispensable tips and a revealing self-assessment exercise that will highlight your strengths and weaknesses, guiding you to improve your performance and attain excellence.

# DEVELOPING YOUR POTENTIAL

To achieve excellence, you must work to fulfill your own potential. Learn to build on your strengths and to develop the personal qualities that are the keys to performing well.

# BUILDING KEY ATTRIBUTES

*Human beings have many talents that can be turned into engines of success. Yet the best performance requires more than mere talent: it involves developing a number of important personal strengths, including determination, vision, and confidence.*

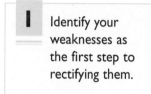

**1** Identify your weaknesses as the first step to rectifying them.

**2** Do things the easy way – play to your strengths.

**3** Accept critical comments and act to remedy faults.

## ASSESSING YOURSELF

You know what comes easily to you, and these strengths can be developed fairly rapidly. Yet your natural powers may not be enough. To reach your full potential, you need to develop all the key attributes. For example, a lack of confidence is a general barrier to advancing in business management. If you are someone who has feelings of low self-esteem, or you lack the courage of your convictions, you will have to work hard to maximize your self-confidence. Begin your self-development by looking objectively at your abilities and where they most need to be improved.

## EVALUATING YOUR KEY ATTRIBUTES

| ATTRIBUTE | HOW TO ASSESS YOURSELF |
| --- | --- |
| AMBITION | Have you written down high and stretching targets and planned how you are going to achieve them? |
| VISION | Have you formed a clear idea of where you want to be and what you want to be doing in five years' time? |
| CONFIDENCE | Do you feel able to do anything that is needed now, do it well, and master new abilities and tasks as required? |
| ABILITY TO TAKE RISKS | Do you believe in your own ability to judge a risk as worth taking and to take your chances effectively? |
| DRIVE AND ENERGY | Can you bring full mental powers to bear on an issue, to decide on the right action, and see it through? |
| COMPETITIVE SPIRIT | Are you never satisfied until you have clearly won all the prizes against the best competition around? |
| SELF-CRITICISM | Are you a relentless perfectionist who constantly seeks to improve and to get others to do the same? |
| LEADERSHIP | Can you mobilize others to achieve group ambitions, as well as develop other leaders and bring them forward? |

# ASKING OTHERS

If you are unsure how you rate in a particular area, such as your ability to lead, get objective feedback from somebody else. Once you have all the facts, you can create a vision of where you want to be in the future. Draw up a mission plan of how to get there.

*Trusted colleague provides objective feedback*

### GETTING FEEDBACK ▶
*Ask a mentor, colleague, or friend to check whether you have exaggerated your strengths or underplayed your weaknesses.*

**TAKE CONTROL**
Lead your own team or take greater responsibility.

**GAIN EXPERIENCE**
Seek to develop and expand your leadership skills.

**SEEK MORE RESPONSIBILITY**
Ensure that you are given responsibility for others.

**BROADEN SKILLS**
Take a position that will widen your knowledge.

**FIND POSITION**
Get a job that will give you the experience you need.

**GET QUALIFICATIONS**
Study for a further qualification that will assist you in reaching your goal.

# CREATING A VISION

Once you have assessed yourself and have a realistic understanding of your abilities, you need to form a vision of significant but attainable aims. The great men and women of history all had a sense of vision and mission. They knew where they were going, what they wanted to achieve, and had the power of direction to help take them to their destination. You can mobilize the same power. Ask yourself where you want to be at the end of each decade that lies ahead. Compare that future vision with where you are now. That shows the gap that must be crossed to realize the vision. The next step is to make closing that gap your overriding mission.

◀ **ACHIEVING YOUR VISION**
*Your mission should be broken down into a feasible operating plan that will enable you to take concrete, achievable steps towards realizing your ultimate goals. Keep both vision and mission firmly before your eyes, with revision as and when required, and direct your actions toward attaining them.*

# IDENTIFYING YOUR MISSION

Now write a hard-headed plan, setting out what you must achieve to realize your vision. The plan must be timed and translated into numbers or hard facts. For example, if your vision is to move into management, your mission might be to acquire the necessary knowledge in year one, join a task force and gain general experience in year two, and obtain a management appointment, inside or outside the company, in year three.

**4** Form long-term ambitions to help you notice chances to move forward.

# MOVING FORWARD

To help you on the path to achieving your vision, you may find it useful to employ the Japanese techniques of *kaizen* and *kaikaku,* or continuous improvement and radical change. *Kaizen* involves constantly looking for ways to improve any element of your performance, like athletes do when they seek to raise their Personal Best (PB). *Kaikaku* takes place less often. It could be going into business for yourself, moving to a new job in a new industry or new company, or both. Look out for opportunities for radical change, and use them.

**5** Take responsibility at the earliest opportunity.

**6** Have targets for both achievement and career moves.

**7** Never be afraid to learn and use the lessons of your failures.

## LOOKING AHEAD

It is far more useful to concentrate on goals achieved and future opportunities than on missed chances. If you miss an opportunity, do not waste time on regrets, but examine why it was ignored or rejected. For example, if you conclude that you lacked the confidence to take a risk, you must develop the confidence to act swiftly next time.

## COMPARING VISIONS AT DIFFERENT CAREER STAGES

**SENIOR MANAGER**
At this level, your vision for yourself goes hand-in-hand with a vision of what your organization can become. You see the road from where the organization is now to this future goal, and you envisage yourself playing a key part, maybe the leading one, in the journey.

**UNIT MANAGER**
You have a clear vision for the success of your unit and an ambitious idea of your own position five years on after achieving that vision.

**FIRST LINE MANAGER**
You now have responsibility for others and envisage developing your people skills and building the business experience that will take you upward.

**FIRST JOB EMPLOYEE**
Your vision is personal. You envisage yourself acquiring the knowledge, experience, and skills needed for advancement in the shortest possible time.

# DEVELOPING CONFIDENCE

*Confidence in yourself and in your abilities is an essential attribute. You can develop self-confidence through experience and training, just as you can learn to use your self-assurance to "sell yourself" when seeking to impress others.*

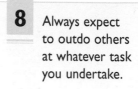

**8** Always expect to outdo others at whatever task you undertake.

## GETTING FEEDBACK

**ASK YOUR SUPERIOR**
*How well am I doing my job? Am I developing abilities that will earn promotion?*

*Manager*

**ASK YOUR PEER**
*Do I help you to do your job better? Am I an effective member of the team?*

*Colleague*

**ASK YOUR SUBORDINATE**
*Do I give you the support you need? Can I do anything different?*

*Employee*

## DOING YOUR BEST

You can strengthen your confidence by dwelling on what you do well. Do not compare yourself unfavorably with others, or suppose that others are judging you adversely. If you do feel inadequate in any area, train to improve your skills. Take pride in what you have done well, and approach your tasks like a professional athlete: train to improve strengths and eliminate weaknesses, but recognize that doing as well as you can, and constantly raising that level, is the most that you (and others) can expect.

## SEEKING ADVICE

People continually observe and frequently judge what you are doing and how – think of yourself as an advertisement that is always "on air." Being scrutinized by others may feel uncomfortable, but your confidence will improve if you know that the observations are positive. Do not be afraid to seek feedback from customers, employers, superiors, colleagues, and suppliers. Having received the feedback, act on what you have learned. This is not the same as seeking the approval of others. You are using their informed and critical advice to improve your performance and thus to feel better about yourself. Take criticisms on board – but do not allow others to damage your self-esteem.

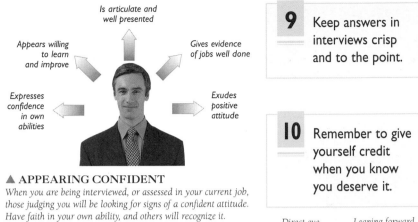

Is articulate and
well presented

Appears willing
to learn
and improve

Gives evidence
of jobs well done

Expresses
confidence
in own
abilities

Exudes
positive
attitude

**9** Keep answers in
interviews crisp
and to the point.

**10** Remember to give
yourself credit
when you know
you deserve it.

▲ **APPEARING CONFIDENT**
*When you are being interviewed, or assessed in your current job, those judging you will be looking for signs of a confident attitude. Have faith in your own ability, and others will recognize it.*

# HANDLING INTERVIEWS

You want to make a confident impression at interviews, whichever side of the table you occupy. For example, whether interviewing an applicant for a job, or applying yourself, you should be neatly attired. Where possible, prepare for the meeting as you would for a speech. Read background information, compile a list of the questions you want to cover, even rehearse especially important points. Seek to end the interview with a definitive summary.

**MAKING A GOOD IMPRESSION** ▶
*It is easier to look confident if you are confident. You should be, provided that you know your subject and are aware of your abilities. Feeling nervous does not mean that you have no confidence; a total lack of anxiety indicates overconfidence.*

Direct eye
contact shows
confidence

Leaning forward
indicates eagerness

Hand
movements
are free and
expressive

**11** Mentally rehearse how you want
an interview to go, and compare
that with what does happen.

# MASTERING RISK-TAKING

*To make significant gains, you must take risks. Confidence and courage are required, as is the ability to look in all directions before you leap. But those who can learn to think, act, and build businesses like entrepreneurs have golden futures.*

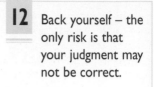

**12** Back yourself – the only risk is that your judgment may not be correct.

**13** Never let an opportunity pass, but think twice before acting.

## HAVING COURAGE

Being entrepreneurial means believing in your own ability and being brave enough to risk being wrong. When dealing with risk, try to think like an entrepreneur: calculate whether a risk is worthwhile, and if it is, have the courage and self-confidence to take it. You can take advice all along the line. But the ultimate "go/no-go" decision is yours alone. If you can take it confidently, then you are being an entrepreneurial manager.

## BEING POSITIVE

Any decision, from starting an enterprise to accepting a new job, has an upside and a potential downside. When facing any risk, adopt the best mental attitude and concentrate on the positive potential, the upside. But be aware that there is always a downside. Even the most gung-ho person considers, even if subconsciously, what will happen if the worst comes to the worst. If the downside is personally unacceptable, look for ways of limiting the risk – ideally a fail-safe position.

▲ **ACCEPTING THE DOWNSIDE**
*Before taking a risk, such as relocating to a new a job, decide whether you can accept the downside. If the downside is unacceptable, for example you cannot face selling your family home, look at all the feasible ways of limiting that risk.*

# CALCULATING RISK

Do not be misled by the old investment maxim that says "the higher the return, the greater the risk." In fact, the upside on a relatively safe move, such as changing jobs, can be very great. However, you must always calculate the risk before taking it, by doing a few simple yet effective calculations. Remember, too, that doing nothing may involve a hidden risk. If you do not make a decision, you might fail to make a breakthrough, either in your career, financially, or in business. If you fail to spot this concealed risk, you will suffer the consequences.

**14** Use lists of pros and cons to test your feelings.

**15** Do your research, and avoid taking action before you have all the facts.

▼ **RISKING A JOB MOVE**
*Work out the likelihood of getting what you want if you move. Next, rate the likelihood of realizing your hopes in your present job. If moving gains a higher total score, the risk is justified.*

*List your criteria for job satisfaction separately*

*Be objective with your scoring*

| Factors | Importance (score out of 10) | Likelihood (score out of 10) | Risk (multiply scores) |
|---|---|---|---|
| **IF I MOVE** | | | |
| Better financial reward | 10 | 10 | 100 |
| Greater opportunity to lead | 5 | 6 | 30 |
| More congenial job | 5 | 5 | 25 |
| Better location | 4 | 8 | 32 |
| **TOTAL** | | | **187** |
| | | | |
| **IF I STAY** | | | |
| Better financial reward | 10 | 5 | 50 |
| Greater opportunity to lead | 5 | 7 | 35 |
| More congenial job | 5 | 5 | 25 |
| Better location | 4 | 4 | 16 |
| **TOTAL** | | | **126** |

# DEVELOPING DRIVE

*You need physical energy to do any job well. But the energy that makes the difference between success and failure is in the mind. You can generate drive by determinedly and persistently channeling your energy toward a chosen purpose.*

**16** Put ambitions on paper so that you can view them as practical plans.

## BEING DETERMINED

It is only human to have grand ideas that you never turn into reality, yet ambitious plans are often perfectly viable. What is lacking is the willpower to activate them. Keep ideas alive by planning action – having the right mind-set will help to draw your attention to valuable observations that you might otherwise miss. Only abandon your plans because analysis has revealed their faults, not because mental laziness or fear have stopped you in your tracks.

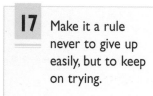

**17** Make it a rule never to give up easily, but to keep on trying.

## MASTERING MIND-SET

**D**rive and energy suggest physical attributes. It is true that, just as some people are born with greater physical powers, so certain psychological gifts are innate. But there is a critical similarity between the physical and the mental. Everybody can choose and reach a target for personal success. By concentrating on that objective, you will generate drive toward achieving the end. You can multiply your energy by channeling it toward the purpose on which your mind is set.

**SETTING A TARGET ▶**
*Everybody can set themselves a target for, say, running faster, which can be reached by training. Even though most people will never even approach the speed of real athletes, their performance can still improve markedly.*

# SEEING IT THROUGH

There are times when giving up is the right policy. But it can work like a self-fulfilling prophecy. Because you are willing to stop, the activity stops, whether it is learning a new language or starting a new business. Many people stop short of their full potential by abandoning a project before reaching their original goal. It may still be within reach, in which case you should carry on. On the other hand, everybody knows examples of people fruitlessly chasing impossible targets. Before deciding to give up, analyze the possible outcomes. If the upside still greatly exceeds the downside, mobilize your drive and energy to pursue the desired conclusion.

 When one goal is achieved, set a new, higher one.

 Imitate somebody with drive and energy to develop those qualities.

## ASSESSING YOUR DRIVE QUOTIENT

Read through the statements below to see which describe you best. If you agree with most statements on the left, your driving ambition is very high. The more statements you agree with on the right, the harder you need to work on developing your drive.

- You see yourself as a younger person.
- You are stable, calm, adventurous, socially bold, confident, and self-assured.
- You have a high need for achievement.
- You welcome change as positive.
- You have a sense of freedom and feel that you are going somewhere.
- You enjoy taking calculated risks.
- You spend a lot of time with superiors.
- Your career has proved more successful than you originally hoped.
- You are willing to move.
- You are rarely ill or absent from work.
- Stress and tension do not affect you.
- You do not smoke and you get exercise.

- You see yourself as an older person.
- You are emotional, shy, restrained, apprehensive, and worry too much.
- You have a low need for achievement.
- You do not like change.
- You feel as though you are locked in, stagnating, and going nowhere.
- You always play it safe.
- You spend no time with superiors.
- Your career has proved less successful than you originally hoped.
- You are unwilling to move.
- You are often ill or absent from work.
- You often feel stressed and tense.
- You smoke and you do not get exercise.

# LEADING EFFECTIVELY

*T he ability to lead others is a prime attribute. To fulfill your leadership potential, learn how to get people to work with you and for you productively, using their initiative for better results. You also need to develop leaders among your staff.*

**20** Avoid asking others to do anything you would not do yourself.

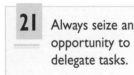

**21** Always seize an opportunity to delegate tasks.

### ENCOURAGING PARTICIPATION ▼

*Bringing competent employees to the fore is a leader's prime task. Allow others to take the initiative whenever possible, encouraging them to contribute their own suggestions and ideas.*

## MANAGING OTHERS

To get the best from people who are working for you, it is essential to set a credible example yourself. Employees will excel themselves for somebody in whose strength and wisdom they truly believe. They also expect professional competence, part of which includes delegating tasks in order to increase staff members' self-management and participation. Ascertain where your employees' strengths and weaknesses lie, then delegate responsibilities that will both exploit these strengths and meet the organization's needs.

*Employee feels encouraged to use own initiative*

*Colleague feels free to put forward ideas*

*Team member feels involved and motivated*

*Manager takes a back seat during meeting*

# WINNING COOPERATION

Cooperation between a manager and his or her staff requires commitment from both sides. If you expect cooperation, you must also give it, while still remaining in overall control. Two key questions to ask your staff are: "What do I do that stops you from doing a better job?" and "What can I do to help you perform better?" If you co-operate by acting on their answers, for example by investing in new tools or training if requested, you can bring about major improvements in performance. Not acting on that feedback will have an adverse effect. Your main objective as leader is to help staff to help themselves.

**22** Actively seek feedback on your own effectiveness.

**23** Always remember that leaders are only as good as those they lead.

## QUESTIONS TO ASK YOURSELF

Q  Do I give others the chance to speak, rather than invariably put forward my own ideas?

Q  Am I loyal to my staff when representing them, both inside and outside the organization?

Q  Do I avoid getting involved in office politics?

Q  Do I strive to achieve a positive atmosphere, in which people compete with ideas?

# DEVELOPING LEADERS

As a manager, you must ensure that you receive the requisite training to develop prioritizing, progress-chasing, delegation, and motivating skills. Make these an integral part of your personal development plan, and ensure that staff members – especially your deputies – also develop their own leadership skills. Listening carefully, criticizing constructively, being tolerant of error while correcting mistakes, and retaining objectivity are all vital leadership qualities. In seeking to develop your own potential, you should also be helping others to develop theirs.

## BUILDING LEADERSHIP SKILLS

All leaders need strong personality traits to assert influence and function. They must also have the ability to facilitate and inspire. To lead others well, you must:

● Ensure that everyone is working toward agreed, shared objectives;

● Criticize constructively, praising merit as well as finding fault;

● Encourage the generation of new ideas;

● Insist on the highest standards;

● Develop individual and team skills and strengthen them by training.

# STAYING IN SHAPE

*Fitness has many dimensions. It is unfair to yourself to expect peak performance at work when your mind and body are in poor shape. Your lifestyle and the amount of exercise you get will affect both your potential and your achievement.*

**24** Measure your fitness and get exercise to raise that level.

## MAINTAINING HEALTH

The majority of people need to make only minimal adjustments to their lifestyle to improve their fitness and maintain the good health that is essential for effective performance. Getting adequate rest, eating a balanced diet, and getting regular exercise are all wise policies, and beneficial in themselves. By leading a balanced lifestyle and looking after your physical wellbeing, you will find that you have a great deal more stamina and energy to achieve your potential at work.

◀ **IMPROVING FITNESS**
*Cycling is a great form of exercise; but to improve your level of fitness you need to set yourself targets. Aim to increase your speed over a known distance, and you will soon feel the benefits.*

## EXERCISING THE BODY

Any fitness program should give you a measured standard of fitness. The best standard is aerobic fitness, which measures the efficiency of the heart and lungs. Some sports, such as rowing, require a high level of aerobic fitness. Others, such as cycling and running, can be used to build up your aerobic fitness gradually, by slowly increasing your speed over a set distance. Choose a sport that you enjoy and set yourself targets for improvement. You will soon feel the benefits, both physically and mentally.

**25** Find a fitness regime you enjoy and that makes you feel good.

## ACHIEVING FITNESS

| SPORT | RECOMMENDED FREQUENCY | AEROBIC VALUE |
| --- | --- | --- |
| CYCLING | 30–45 minutes, three times a week. | Very high |
| ROWING | 3 hours, once a week | Very high |
| RUNNING | 30–45 minutes, three times a week | Very high |
| SWIMMING | 45 minutes, three times a week | Very high |
| SOCCER | 1–2 hours, twice a week | High |
| WALKING | 45 minutes, three times a week | High |
| SQUASH | 1 hour, twice a week | Medium |
| TENNIS | 1–2 hours, twice a week | Medium |
| VOLLEYBALL | 1–2 hours, twice a week | Medium |
| GOLF | 36 holes, once a week | Low |

**26** Combine aerobic value with ways of exercising all the key muscles.

**27** Do not patiently tolerate pain, but obtain advice about its cause and cure.

## STAYING NIMBLE

Aerobic fitness is by no means the only standard. Balance, flexibility, and strength are other, often neglected aspects of fitness. You can improve these by working out in a gym. But you can help yourself a great deal by simply walking briskly, bending, stretching, sitting and standing straight, and so on. Spending 10 minutes a day on suitable stretching exercises, including yoga and t'ai chi, is highly beneficial. If you still end up with aches and pains, they may be work-related – for example, if you slouch at your desk, you may well be straining your back. In such cases, osteopathy and similar therapies can produce miraculous results.

# EATING FOR FITNESS

Your food gives you vital nutrients for health and calories for energy. Business life offers many temptations that work against eating sensibly, and the snatched sandwich at the desk, lunchtime drinking, and expense account feasts can all have bad effects on the concentration, the digestion, and the waistline. Have a target weight, keep to it by controling your calories, and take a vitamin supplement as insurance against missing nutrients.

▲ **EATING HEALTHILY**
*No matter how busy you are, make time for breakfast. Cereals or bread and fresh fruit or juices give you the energy you need to start the day.*

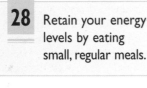

**28** Retain your energy levels by eating small, regular meals.

**29** Never ignore any symptom of stress – get treatment.

# SEEKING HELP

The stresses and strains of working life can trigger breakdowns, ranging from minor depression to total collapse. The solution is the same as for any physical symptoms: if you feel that your mental fitness is being significantly impaired, get advice. Simply talking to a friend or to your doctor may provide enough help. Pharmaceutical drugs can help, while alternative therapies, such as meditation, have their place, too. But suffering in silence will reduce your performance and may eventually devastate your ability to work.

## AVOIDING DEPRESSION

The more you agree with these statements, the more likely it is your mental health is good. The more you disagree, the more likely you are to be suffering mild depression or worse:

- I do not feel at all unhappy.
- I am optimistic about the future.
- I do not feel a failure.
- I am fairly satisfied with life.
- I do not feel particularly guilty.
- I have no thoughts of harming myself.
- I am not disappointed with myself.
- I am interested in other people.
- I make decisions as well as ever.
- I look as good as I used to.
- I can work as well as ever.
- I do not get more tired than usual.
- My appetite is as good as ever.
- I do not overindulge.

▲ **GETTING AWAY**
*Vacationing with your family or friends allows you to get away from the pressures of your daily routine and work-related stress. A number of short breaks can be more refreshing than rare, longer vacations. Take every opportunity, including staying extra days or combining business trips with a day or so of relaxation.*

## POINTS TO REMEMBER

● Arranging flexible working hours may help you to avoid traveling to work during busy, peak times.

● Cycling or walking to work a few times a week will improve fitness.

● Eating small meals at regular intervals is better than indulging in one enormous dinner.

● Relaxing before going to bed by reading, watching television, or listening to music will improve the quality of your sleep.

● Making sure that people at work are aware of your commitments to your family will help to generate understanding when you need to take time off, such as for your child's sports day.

## TAKING BREAKS

Some people who have built exceptional careers work "all the hours in the day," sometimes in the belief that this gives them a winning edge over those who put in fewer hours. Success, though, depends on the strength of ideas and their execution, neither of which has much to do with the time expended. Overwork, on the other hand, can adversely affect both thinking and performance. Try to avoid taking work home (or going into the office) on weekends. To perform well, you must lead a well-balanced life and schedule time off.

## SLEEPING WELL

Sleep is indispensable to good performance. While the hours needed vary from person to person, everybody requires a minimum dose. The requirement can be deliberately reduced. By cutting down sleeping time gradually over a long period, you can reach the probable minimum of four hours, freeing that time for other activities. If you lose sleep without training, though, the results will be cumulative and counterproductive, especially if you do not take catnaps during the day.

**30** If you are feeling tired, try to take a short catnap – it will prove highly restorative.

# PURSUING EXCELLENCE

*There is no good alternative to the goal of perfectionism – seeking top performance in yourself, and being constantly dissatisfied at less-than-perfect results. Be your own best critic, drawing attention to your faults, and going in search of excellence.*

 **31** Seek excellence, and do not stop at "good" – it is not good enough.

## QUESTIONS TO ASK YOURSELF

Q Do I rate the quality of my performance every day?

Q Am I working on a method that will improve results?

Q Do I take criticism from others and react well to it?

Q Do I meet the standards that I demand from others?

Q Do I remind myself of what I did well in the past?

## SEEKING PERFECTION

The pursuit of the highest possible standards automatically points you toward achieving excellence. If you achieve perfection in any activity, you must be the best, which is the proper objective in any context. Even momentary perfection is extremely hard to achieve, if not impossible. In practice, aiming for excellence will mean performing significantly better than your present standards, which are always imperfect. Remember that refusal to tolerate imperfection is a powerful force for success.

## BEING THE BEST

Just like runners, managers and organizations need opponents, or at least pacesetters, to produce their best performance. The process known as "benchmarking" measures comparable performance to set targets that the company seeks to exceed. The defect in this approach is that the benchmarks may themselves be too low. You want to be the best at what you do. That means looking at the performance of others to see not just what they do well, but how it could be dramatically improved. Being the best means setting new standards, very likely by adopting new methods. This drive for reform can be very demanding, but also highly rewarding.

 **32** Assume that you can always find a better way to use your abilities.

 **33** Aim at perfection, even if that seems impossibly out of reach.

## BEING SELF-CRITICAL

There is a crucial difference between self-criticism and low self-esteem. You need a high personal opinion of your aptitudes and the way that you apply them. But you first earn that high personal regard by subjecting your actions and output to rigorous judgment. By acting as your own most severe critic, you avoid complacency and substitute the pursuit of excellence. Just as with others, it is important to make constructive, rather than negative criticisms, and then take positive action to improve areas of weakness. Beware if you find nothing to criticize, however. That is usually a sign of trouble ahead.

**34** Welcome new tasks as tests that you will pass.

**35** On completing any work, rank your performance out of 100 – strictly.

## RAISING YOUR STANDARDS

However good you are at something, you can always improve. Similarly, however high the standards you have set for yourself and others, they can always be raised higher. Apply the total quality principle of continuous improvement to everything that you do. When starting a new job, you may feel daunted by new demands and doubt your ability to tackle the tasks successfully. Yet your past experience will confirm that after a few weeks in the new role, you will be performing well and without difficulty. People tend to underestimate their powers, which achieves the opposite of maximizing potential. It is better to overshoot and miss than never to try for the best of which you are capable.

▼ **IMPROVING STANDARDS**
*Seek constantly to improve your performance by consistently setting yourself new and higher personal targets, and by taking every possible opportunity to learn and practice new skills.*

*Increase your skills by taking advantage of one-on-one training courses, where possible*

## ACCEPTING CHALLENGES

You may be happy doing the same work in the same role for years. However, that is extremely unlikely to represent your full potential. Restlessness is a good sign and a valuable quality. Once a task has been successfully completed, you look for new pastures and challenges. Be biased in favor of accepting these challenges when offered. You have a limited number of years in your career, and it makes sense to move onward and preferably upward whenever you can. This kind of restlessness has nothing to do with dissatisfaction or "itchy feet." It is simply the desire to test your powers in new situations – an angle that should always be followed.

> **36** Do not become a hard taskmaster, but do be a demanding one who helps others to work well.

### WELCOMING COMPETITION

You should always welcome competition because it has a positive effect. Lack of competition tends to stultify. Conversely, the urge to outdo the opposition by fair and square means will powerfully stimulate drive and energy, in individuals and organizations alike. Foster that urge, in yourself and your team, by all available means. Choose the best "enemy" you can and make them the one to beat, and their standards the ones to exceed. But keep the aggression under careful, directed control.

## INSPIRING EXCELLENCE

Seeking perfection for yourself entitles you to make similar demands of others. Part of your own drive for excellence aims to achieve maximum potential in others. Harness their innate desire to be committed, to excel, to seek responsibility, and to use their mental powers by setting an excellent example yourself. Spur people on to seek excellence by encouraging and rewarding them when they produce outstanding results.

▲ **HELPING OTHERS TO EXCEL**
*Help people to reach the high standards you set by giving them the coaching they need to perform to their best ability. Ensure that you reward and encourage people when they do excel.*

# PURSUING EXCELLENCE IN THE KEY ATTRIBUTES

| ATTRIBUTES | HOW TO ACHIEVE EXCELLENCE |
|---|---|
| **AMBITION**<br>Willingness to take initiatives to reach high targets. | ● Aim for the "impossible" – it has often been achieved.<br>● Translate your ambitions into concrete time-scales.<br>● Regard financial reward as a result of achieving worthwhile, major ambitions, not as an end in itself. |
| **VISION**<br>Keeping long-term, future success as a constant guide. | ● Never allow the problems of the present to make you forget that there is a future for which to plan.<br>● Share your vision with others and seek their support.<br>● Review the vision periodically and revise as needed. |
| **CONFIDENCE**<br>The conviction that you can achieve what you want to do. | ● If you feel inadequate for a particular task, take immediate steps to obtain any training, etc. you need.<br>● Do not hesitate to ask for advice from others.<br>● Do not allow criticism to damage your self-esteem. |
| **ABILITY TO TAKE RISKS**<br>Readiness to take chances rather than play safe. | ● Consider the downside and upside of any decision.<br>● Never gamble, but make the best judgment you can of the probabilities: aim for highest return at lowest risk.<br>● Test your hunches, but do not be afraid to back them. |
| **DRIVE AND ENERGY**<br>The ability to concentrate mental and physical powers. | ● Be determined and persevere in reaching your goals.<br>● Devote your drive and energy to planning as well as action, and take steps to maintain the momentum.<br>● React forcefully to failure and reinforce success. |
| **COMPETITIVE SPIRIT**<br>Relentless perfectionism in seeking to be the best. | ● Identify your main competition and make it a target.<br>● Never be content with second best – strive for first.<br>● Combine constant small improvements in performance with periodic leaps forward through major change. |
| **SELF-CRITICISM**<br>Facing up to mistakes and failures, and learning from them. | ● Avoid blaming others for anything that goes wrong.<br>● Make a habit of conducting a calm postmortem to analyze the reasons for error and remove causes.<br>● If things go really well, rejoice in your success. |
| **LEADERSHIP**<br>The ability to mobilize others to achieve group ambitions. | ● Remember that bringing other leaders to the fore is a prime task of leadership and a highway to success.<br>● Lead from the front, but not by doing others' jobs.<br>● Show strength by consultation and taking advice. |

# IMPROVING YOUR SKILLS

Whatever stage you have reached in your career, it is vital to keep learning. By widening and applying your knowledge, you can dramatically improve your performance.

## INCREASING LEARNING

*You are never too old to learn, and the need for learning increases, rather than decreases, as your career advances and jobs become more complex and important. Time for study may be hard to find, but it always pays off.*

**37** If you feel you need to have more training, ask for what you require.

**38** Learn new skills that are not linked to work demands.

**39** Never think that training is now all behind you.

### EDUCATING YOURSELF

Many people promoted to a new, senior position think that they can learn on the job, without any need for education in the new tasks. Yet, if you wanted to indulge in a new hobby, for example wind-surfing, you would expect to take lessons. The same principle applies to taking up a new position or moving to a new company. Your natural ability needs reinforcement by learning, in both general and specific ways, how to do the work. Many companies fail to insist on this reinforcement. If the employer will not provide the learning, take steps to get it yourself.

# LEARNING A LANGUAGE

Mastering other tongues makes a difference in negotiations and business relationships. It is also a valuable exercise for the mind. Cassettes and videos are effective learning tools – but the best learning is interactive. You can sign up for classes or use interactive media. Then, take every chance to use your new skill. It will impress everybody, including your foreign business contacts.

*Manager uses cassettes to master a new language*

**APPLYING YOURSELF ▶**
*Set aside regular study periods and find a quiet environment where you can concentrate on learning without being distracted.*

# MASTERING COMPUTERS

However you obtain access to computing power, it is an indispensable extension of your own brain and capabilities. You must quickly master a word-processing program, email, and a spreadsheet. Productivity aids like engagement calendars and personal databases, too, are worth their weight in gold and cost little (in some cases, nothing). Apart from the personal benefits they bring, computers in many organizations now provide essential access to company files, colleagues, messages, customers, suppliers, collaborative working, and the Internet (which will be, and in many cases already is, the conduit to these contacts).

**▲ REAPING THE BENEFITS**
*Computer programs may take time and effort to master, but the investment will be returned many times over. It is important to make that investment.*

# USING YOUR KNOWLEDGE

Make sure that any courses you plan to attend are relevant to your work. Then do all you can to apply what you have learned. Do not be deterred by less enlightened colleagues who may pour scorn on what you have been taught. You can only discover whether those lessons have real value by putting them into practice in your day-to-day work. Pass on your new knowledge to colleagues, and make them your allies.

**40** Insist on getting training you can use, and then insist on using it.

# EFFECTIVE THINKING

*The most important mental discipline – thinking – is the one least taught in schools or in organizations. You can improve your thinking by using logic and by adopting proven techniques that will lead to better understanding, ideas, and execution.*

**41** Acquire all the information you need before you draw conclusions.

*Assess all the facts before planning action*

▲ **PLANNING LOGICALLY**
*Write down what is likely to happen and the potential ramifications; then you can plan how to deal with each eventuality.*

## USING YOUR LOGIC

Logic means correct reasoning. Use your logic and you will reach the ideal stage where the compelling force of the facts eliminates all alternatives except one. This cannot happen all the time, because there will be too many unknowns. But the rational manager starts by seeking factual certainty, from which he or she can proceed to firm conclusions. Logic is no less invaluable in uncertain conditions. You can list possible events and logically establish what consequences will follow if they occur. You can then produce sensible plans for coping with each possibility, and also work out the relative likelihoods. Logic also teaches that the best-laid plans may go wrong, so cover this contingency in your thinking.

## THINKING LATERALLY

Lateral thinking, as taught by Edward de Bono, uses various techniques to make you challenge received ideas and arrive at new, improved solutions and suggestions. One such technique is provocation, when you put forward outlandish notions to see what practical ideas are stimulated as a result. Another approach is to seek analogies from other fields. If you are told that something is impossible or will never work, redouble your efforts to see if the idea is, in fact, valuable.

**42** Do not confuse wild, far-out, impractical ideas with creativity.

# BACKING YOUR INTUITION

Hunch or gut feeling sound far less impressive than logic, lateral thinking, and reasoning. But intuitive thought-processes are as intellectual as any other. Intuition may take into account factors that your consciousness wants to repress, which is why some indefinable doubt may prevent you from making a decision. Never ignore such messages from the interior. But treat intuitive thoughts as analytically as logical plans. Check the intuition against the facts. You may not always establish a complete case for backing your instincts. Going with it in these circumstances may well be the best course – so long as you can stand the consequences of being wrong.

**43** Encourage people in thinking sessions to give full rein to their intuition as well as their logic.

## QUESTIONS TO ASK YOURSELF

Q Have I gathered all the facts I need to help me arrive at the correct solution?

Q Have I considered all possible alternatives before settling on my decision?

Q Have I gone out of my way to find new methods of tackling this situation?

Q Did I collect contributions from everybody who has an interest in the matter?

Q Have I used the best possible thinking process in reaching my conclusion?

Q What do I feel about the matter – am I convinced emotionally as well as intellectually?

Q Have I thought of contingency plans in case my ideas do not work out as intended?

## TACKLING ▶ ISSUES LOGICALLY

*When you apply reasoning to a situation, the result can be counterintuitive – that is, not what you would expect. In this case, David's intuition was to cut prices to stimulate sales performance. But his boss wanted to probe deeper. His logical analysis showed that the firm would be far worse off as the result of cutting prices. The sales chief's intuitive proposal was not a good one.*

### CASE STUDY

David, sales chief of a large organization, was concerned about sales trends. He approached his managing director, John, with a proposal to cut prices by 20 percent to stimulate sales. He told John that sales would fall steeply if the price cut did not go through, but would rise sharply if it did. John figured out how much sales would have to rise to cover the lost profit. The answer was fivefold! He then went on to calculate how much sales would have to fall if prices rose by 20 percent, before profits were affected. The figure worked out at 44 percent. He put the analysis before David and asked, "Do you really believe that a 20-percent price differential will raise sales by 400 percent?". Reluctantly, David said no.

# IMPROVING MEMORY

*A good memory is a great asset, and one that can always be developed. Even the most amazing memory experts rely on acquired techniques to perform their feats. Follow similar approaches, and you will never forget what you need to remember.*

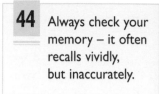

**44** Always check your memory – it often recalls vividly, but inaccurately.

## TESTING MEMORY

**45** Take training in how to recall if your memory is letting you down.

People often complain that their memory is failing, but recall is affected by factors, including stress and fatigue, that do not reflect intellectual capability. Try a simple test. Can you, for example, remember a list of ten items in the correct order after one read-through? If you cannot, do not despair. A little training will show that your memory power can accomplish this and many more complex tasks.

## REMEMBERING LISTS AND NUMBERS

To help you remember a list, try composing a story that includes all the items. The more outlandish it is, the better. For example: "A man needs **aspirin** for a bad headache after drinking too much **wine** which cost too much **money**. He makes a **note** in his **pad** never to do it again, and starts eating **oranges** as a cure. One of the oranges **flowers** and turns into a tree, which is pulped to make a **book**. The book contains a recipe for cooking cold **sausages** with **soap powder** to make **pet food**." You will now remember the list perfectly.

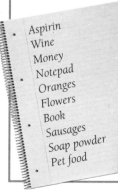

- Aspirin
- Wine
- Money
- Notepad
- Oranges
- Flowers
- Book
- Sausages
- Soap powder
- Pet food

If you find it difficult to remember numbers, try substituting word associations for the digits, for example using simple rhymes: 1= Sun, 2= Shoe, 3= Tree, and so on. In this way, you can compose your own numerical associations. Any list of objects, ideas, people, points in a speech, or numbers can be fixed in the memory by association with your ten "number words."

## USING ASSOCIATION

**B**eing able to remember what you want or need is very valuable. You do not have to leave it to your natural powers. Association is the key to effective memorizing, and by using it deliberately you can easily accomplish feats you would have thought beyond you, such as delivering a 30-minute speech without notes. Association involves linking what you are trying to remember with other things, such as rhymes. Mnemonics are also a form of association, such as "Columbus sailed the ocean blue in fourteen hundred and ninety two."

**46** Develop a good filing system for items you read and want to keep.

## AIDING YOUR MEMORY

**T**here is no reason to burden your head with searching your memory when a computer, filing system, or notebook can do the job perfectly well. You should also keep a large number of reference sites, either on the Internet or your bookshelves. The computer makes all these tasks much easier. But it is up to you to take practical steps to record these "memories."

▼ **STORING INFORMATION**
*Devise a filing system to suit your needs and make sure that it is efficient – you should be able to locate items easily whenever you need to recall them.*

*Keyword identifies contents*

*Simple label is attached to each file*

*Devise an efficient filing system to help you find whatever you want quickly and easily*

*Files are color coded according to subject matter*

◀ **KEEPING RECORDS**
*Write down as soon as possible your notes on an interview, something you have read, the name of a new contact, or information you have been given, and file it away.*

# IMPROVING READING

*Reading is fundamentally important for efficiency. The faster you read, and the more you understand, the better. The view that comprehension suffers with speed is wrong. Learn to read faster, and you will find that understanding also improves.*

**47** Read for useful tips from other businesses and other countries.

## READING MORE QUICKLY

**F**ew managers know a vital personal statistic. How fast do you read now? The average is somewhere between 250 and 300 words per minute (wpm), but you can train yourself, or be trained, to read much faster. The first tip is only to read what you need to read. Survey the material first, eliminate the superfluous, and read only what is essential. Do not go back over words and sentences that you have already read. Keep the eyes moving forwards between groups of words, taking in as many words as possible in each group. By following such easy tips, you can speed up by 30 percent, saving two hours in reading a book of normal length.

*Book is flat on desk*

*Comfortable posture aids concentration*

▲ **SKIM-READING**
*Practice skim-reading from paragraph to paragraph. Read in bursts of about 20 minutes, eliminating distractions.*

## UNDERSTANDING FASTER

**I**n the mistaken belief that reading faster means understanding less, people often reread passages and sentences many times. In fact, their strategy is flawed. Tests show that comprehension rises with increased speed. The trained reader not only manages double the normal speed or more, but also has a higher degree of comprehension. The same methods that raise speed also concentrate the mind more effectively on what is being read. Get into the habit of taking notes. The process of selecting key points itself aids understanding.

**48** Set time targets for your reading and make sure you stick to them.

## CHOOSING A SUBJECT

You probably have plenty to read simply in the course of your job. But that job will be better done if you read much more widely. Set yourself a weekly or monthly reading plan and try to stick to it. You could set a target of at least one good newspaper a day, one relevant magazine a week, and one serious book a month. The book need not be about business management, although excellent works on all its aspects appear every year. Every such book contains valuable lessons, information, and ideas. So do newspapers and magazines. One pizza multimillionaire in the US has the world's biggest library of self-help books. Whether or not these tomes contributed to his success, the principle is powerful. There is much to be gained from reading for self-education. But do not forget to read for relaxation, too – the more you enjoy reading, the less of a chore it becomes.

### THINGS TO DO

1. Test your reading speed and set a faster target.
2. Test your comprehension, reading slowly and fast.
3. Set time aside every day for your reading.
4. Scan books first to see which parts interest you.
5. Have a reading list for books useful in business and for general culture.

### RETAINING YOUR READING

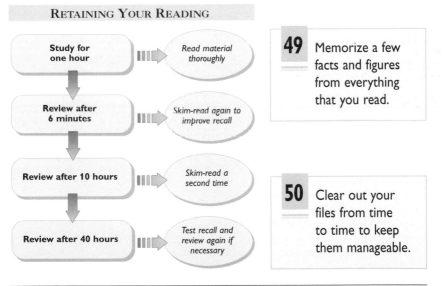

| Study for one hour | ▸ | Read material thoroughly |

| Review after 6 minutes | ▸ | Skim-read again to improve recall |

| Review after 10 hours | ▸ | Skim-read a second time |

| Review after 40 hours | ▸ | Test recall and review again if necessary |

**49** Memorize a few facts and figures from everything that you read.

**50** Clear out your files from time to time to keep them manageable.

# WRITING AND SPEAKING MORE FLUENTLY

Most managers, like most people, find speaking in public and writing well difficult. Obey simple rules and your performance on paper will pass any normal tests, while you also have the potential to be an effective public speaker for any audience.

**51** Get a respected friend to read and criticize your writing.

## WRITING TEXT

Always choose short words over long ones, and active verbs rather than passive ones, when you are producing text. Keep sentences short and to the point. Do not use self-important devices, like capital letters for words that are not proper names, or management jargon. Avoid archaisms like "albeit" or "notwithstanding." Shun clichés like "on-going" or "at this point in time." In addition, seek a smooth flow, with logical transitions from thought to thought and paragraph to paragraph. Never write more words than you need. If you shorten any piece of writing, you will probably improve its quality. It helps throughout to visualize your audience, and to aim your words at that target.

**52** Read all writing aloud or silently to check quality.

*Use symbols for common words, such as th for the, k for thousand*

*Drop all vowels unless they begin a word*

*Words are still easy to recognize when they are spelled without vowels*

*Use numerals for numbers*

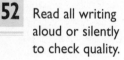

In th sm wy tht spdwrtg ncrss th spd at whch y wrt nts wth a pn or pncl, y cn gtly incrs the spd at whch y mk nts usg a wrd prcssr or typwrtr, if tht is hw y prfr t wrk.

Whn y spdwrt, th shp of th wrds is unffctd by th dltd vwls, & y hv an entrly smpl & prctcl systm.

Y my fnd tht evn whn y ar sklld at spdwrtg, it is snsbl t spll unusual or dffclt wrds in fll. Als, if yr spdwrttn wrd cld b mstkn for 1 or 2 othr wrds, thn it is a gd pln t wrt th wrd in fll.

◀ **TAKING NOTES**
*Space your notes in short paragraphs and concentrate on picking out the main points, facts, and phrases. Try an easy speedwriting system, which can double your speed, by eliminating vowels and using symbols for common words.*

**▲ DICTATING TEXT**
*You will be able to dictate faster if you plan the document beforehand and have all notes and reference material ready. Allocate the time required and keep on to the end before revising your material.*

## DICTATING PROSE

Writing takes considerable time. Only experts can write good prose at 20 words a minute or more. Speaking at 160 words per minute (wpm) is comfortable for you and the listener, so it follows that dictation is the fastest form of writing. You will not reach 160 wpm, of course. But you can easily double or triple your current speed. You will need somebody to take the dictation or transcribe the tape, however, and will also have to find time for revision and rewriting. Computer programs can take dictation, too, but they are not yet perfect.

**53** Practice giving a talk without referring to your notes or using a watch to check elapsed time.

*Look directly at audience and maintain open stance*

*Refer to notes only when necessary*

## SPEAKING CLEARLY

Nearly everybody speaks perfectly well in ordinary life. There are extraordinary orators, but you are not competing in their league. In your everyday conversation, you make your meaning clear, have an easy flow, and cover all the necessary ground without being long-winded. That is all that is required in speaking for your professional purposes. Imagine that you are speaking to a group of friends who, like you, are deeply interested in what you have to say, and whom you do not have to impress with wordiness.

**◀ BEING NATURAL**
*If you are familiar with your notes, you will appear more natural and will be better able to establish a good rapport with the audience.*

## OVERCOMING NERVES

Even professional broadcasters, who look thoroughly at ease on camera, admit to nervousness before a program starts. Even prize-winning authors doubt the quality of their latest writing. Such nervousness reflects a desirable stimulus, setting the adrenaline flowing as you gird yourself for the fight. If you suffer very seriously from nerves, relieve them by using relaxation techniques, going for a short walk, or going over your material. Above all, remember that your audiences and associates generally want you to succeed. They are rarely hostile. They want to be pleased as much as you want to please them.

Breathe in through nose

Feel chest remain still as you inhale

Feel diaphragm rise with each inward breath

▲ REDUCING LAST-MINUTE NERVES
*Try this breathing exercise to calm your thoughts and dispel tension. Close your eyes. Place one hand on your upper chest, the other on your diaphragm. Breathe in, feeling your diaphragm rise, then breathe out slowly. Repeat several times.*

**54** Pick a point in the audience some two-thirds back for eye contact.

**55** Use professional slides presented via a computer for best effect.

## STRUCTURING YOUR TALK

Any talk consists of three Ms: Message, Material, and Manner. What do you want to communicate? Have one overarching, big message you will leave with the audience. Follow the basic sequence of telling the audience what you are going to say (the big message), saying it, and finally repeating what you have said. Within the overall message, write down the key points (as few as possible) in bullet form, and allow about three minutes per point. What will you use to support the message? Write down against each key point the slides, statistics, other facts and stories that you will use. The ideal length is between 20 and 40 minutes. Above that, audiences tend to lose concentration.

# PRESENTING YOUR TALK

How will the message and material be presented? You have a wide choice of styles: roaming the stage or room, delivering from a fixed point, using notes, reading a script (which is rarely advisable), formal or informal, participative or lecturing, and so on. Suit the choice to your own personality and preference, but above all to the audience. Learn as much as you can about what each particular audience expects and likes. Maintain eye contact so that you can judge the impact of your talk and adjust if necessary. Use audio-visual aids if at all possible. Videos, slides, and overheads make the message much more effective and memorable than words alone can achieve.

## ▼ PRESENTING EFFECTIVELY

*Make use of visuals wherever possible, since they are powerful aids; but remember to maintain that all-important eye contact by looking at the audience rather than the screen. Try to inject some humor into the presentation as a means of winning over your audience, and always end on a strong, emphatic note.*

## CULTURAL DIFFERENCES

Americans are fond of moving around while speaking and of trying to become part of the audience. The British are much more likely to use a lectern and to rely quite heavily on audio-visual material. The Japanese can surprise their European or American audiences by giving extremely witty and informal presentations. The Germans, too, can speak humorously, although their humor may be more apparent to German audiences than to other nationalities. The French may be very fluent – even in English.

# BECOMING MORE EFFECTIVE

There are a number of tools and techniques that can be used to raise performance. With a little know-how, you can ensure that you are making maximum use of your personal resources.

## BOOSTING CREATIVITY

*Most people think that creativity is best left to a talented few. They are wrong. Everybody has creative powers and can learn to use them. By opening your mind and changing your approach, you will discover that ideas come easily.*

**56** Expect everybody to have ideas and to express them with no inhibitions.

### BEING INVENTIVE

Many organizations fall into the trap of believing that time-honored ways cannot be bettered, or else they lag behind because they always follow the market leader. Individuals also repeat what has worked in the past, and copy others who have been successful. But to be creative, you have to adopt a different approach. Ask yourself what would happen if you turned existing practices upside down. Or search for something that is not being done at all. People will say "If it was a good idea, somebody else would have done it." Take that as a trigger for investigating further.

**57** Look for innovative ideas that can change things for the better.

# CHANGING APPROACH

In creating your personal and business strategies, do not merely imitate the competition. It may help you to know that from the time of the ancient Greeks to World War II, out of all the major conflicts and numerous campaigns, only six decisive victories followed from head-on assaults. All the other victors launched flanking attacks – they went around the side. Learn from these historical lessons, and look for an idea that will give a clear differentiation. You can then hope to win without the massive advantage in strength needed for head-on success. In this way, small armies have been able to defeat military giants three times their size. Moreover, in doing the same thing, you may do it worse. Be different and set your own standards.

# FINDING IDEAS

Ideas can be found almost anywhere – in other countries, other companies, and other industries. To discover them, you must make reading and observation your tools, and then give full rein to your creative urge to experiment. If you discover a new method or product, you may be able to try it out for a trial period, or in a test market, which allows you to make sure before commitment. "Stolen" ideas are also very valuable, not only in original form but as analogies. By observing or reading, you may find an idea that can be applied successfully in a completely different context.

*Cut out interesting items and refer to them when you need inspiration*

◀ COLLECTING CLIPPINGS
*Magazines, books, and newspapers are invaluable sources of inspiration. Read through them and keep any items of interest so that you build up your own reference library of ideas.*

# Using Time Efficiently

*Time is your most valuable asset, and how well you use it has a key bearing on how you perform. By analyzing how you spend your time, you can begin to make changes that will ensure you get the most from your working day.*

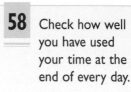

**58** Check how well you have used your time at the end of every day.

**59** List the day's tasks in order of priority, then tackle them one by one.

## Analyzing Use of Time

You might think that most of your time is spent doing useful things, but if you were to keep a detailed time-log, you would probably be surprised at the number of superfluous activities. It is easy to spend too much time on routine matters, such as reading mail, at the expense of high-priority, productive tasks. Look at how you divide your day at the moment. Do you prioritize your work so that you tackle important, urgent projects first? Or do you complete enjoyable tasks first? Do you waste a lot of time?

## Allocating Time

The majority of your tasks can be divided into three groups: routine tasks (for example, writing a regular report), one-off tasks (for example, organizing a meeting), and planning and development tasks (for example, making new contacts). To be most effective in your job, you should be spending about 60 percent of your time on the most important Group 3 tasks, 25 percent on Group 2 tasks, and only 15 percent on Group 1 needs. If, like most people, you allocate your time in exactly the opposite proportions, try to reorganize your working day so that you are able to work more consistently and efficiently, and achieve more.

### Questions to Ask Yourself

Q Am I devoting enough time and resources to strategic planning and overall monitoring?

Q Is my desk overflowing with uncompleted tasks?

Q Do I leave enough time to be creative and innovative?

Q Am I delegating routine but necessary tasks to staff?

Q Do I allocate sufficient time to sourcing new contacts?

Q Am I spending too much time in meetings?

# DELEGATING WORK

**B**y delegating aspects of your work to others, you give yourself time to complete the most important elements of your job successfully. Divide your necessary tasks into three groups: those that do not need to be done at all – by you or anyone else; those that you could and should delegate; and those that you are not able to delegate and must do yourself. Use this breakdown as a basis for reducing any unnecessary activities, delegating more tasks, and concentrating on tasks that only you can complete.

## DECIDING WHAT TO DELEGATE

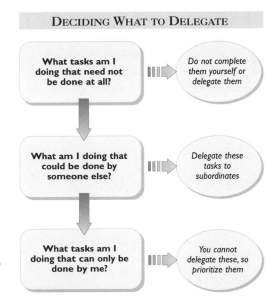

What tasks am I doing that need not be done at all? → *Do not complete them yourself or delegate them*

What am I doing that could be done by someone else? → *Delegate these tasks to subordinates*

What tasks am I doing that can only be done by me? → *You cannot delegate these, so prioritize them*

▲ **USING MOMENTS**
*Make the most of a long journey by writing a report, studying a document, or reading a book or article. Portable computers have made this "stolen" time still more usable.*

# FILLING IN TIME

**L**ong periods of idleness, such as when traveling or waiting for meetings, are wasteful. Always have work available for filling in these times. If you have a long drive to work, why not take the chance to listen to recorded material? If you travel to work by train, use the time to read or plan your day ahead. Advances in communications mean that we can contact the office or talk to colleagues, wherever we are in the world. Make sure you are equipped with the know-how and the tools to take advantage of new technologies.

# BEING MORE PRODUCTIVE

Having efficiently allocated your time, you must ensure that you are being as productive as possible within those time restraints. Find ways of measuring your personal performance, set higher targets, and improve processes to close the gap.

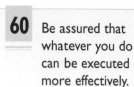

**60** Be assured that whatever you do can be executed more effectively.

## MEASURING OUTPUT

You can always find measures of output and effectiveness. How quickly do you answer your phone? How punctual are you? Do you clear your desk every night? Once you have chosen measures that fit your working pattern, look at the processes you use to see if you can cut out or speed up any stages. People often develop working habits without questioning their effectiveness – if you can change these habits for the better, do so.

**61** Get colleagues to help you sustain improvements in your productivity.

*Manager passes on report, confident of the quality*

## ENSURING QUALITY

Quality is essential. High output at low standards is not productive. For example, responding to letters promptly is worth much less if the letters are badly written, unclear, and inaccurate. The same obvious truth applies to all your work. Take time before beginning any task to decide on the best approach and the objectives – both what you want to achieve and how the work will be presented. It may be wise to put problems on one side, rather than delay the whole work, returning to the difficult areas when the task is broadly finished.

◀ **DOING YOUR BEST**
*Before handing over your work, make sure that you are truly satisfied that it has been well done. Be your own strictest inspector, and always allow enough time for review and revision.*

# MAKING IMPROVEMENTS

One simple way of improving productivity is to concentrate on activities that you control personally, rather than on those that are outside your control. Set yourself new, higher, productivity targets – for example, if you tend to turn up late for meetings, resolve to be punctual every time. Look at the way in which you structure your day in terms of your own productivity. If you know that your energy levels tend to flag during the middle of the afternoon, scheduling an arduous, complicated task for this time of day would not be productive. You might achieve far more by tackling such a complex job early in the morning.

## QUESTIONS TO ASK YOURSELF

Q What are the key measures that relate to my effectiveness?

Q Have I set targets for self-improvement?

Q Am I maximizing my output but limiting my input?

Q Do I keep my desk clear and my papers organized?

Q Am I certain that I am improving performance in measurable ways?

**62** Insist on people making quality a prime target.

## ▼ IMPROVING PRODUCTIVITY

*A clear, well-organized desk and the ability to focus on the task at hand indicate high levels of productivity. Review your working practices regularly, and keep setting yourself new targets to ensure that those high standards are not allowed to slip.*

*Employee concentrates on task at hand*

*Reports are produced swiftly, without compromising quality*

*Paperwork is filed neatly*

*In-tray is cleared regularly*

# CHOOSING PRIORITIES

*Effective time management involves prioritizing. You cannot handle all the tasks that come your way at the same time. Working to a list of priorities is vital. It is also important to give priority to developing your expertise in a chosen area of specialty.*

**63** Put what can wait indefinitely into a file, then throw away the contents.

**64** Try to finish one task before you start on another.

**COMPARING PRIORITIES ▼**
*Look at the way you prioritize carefully. The good prioritizer puts the future ahead of the past and tackles difficult jobs first. The bad prioritizer puts the past before the future and postpones demanding tasks.*

## ASSESSING IMPORTANCE

Tasks fall into four categories: very important, important, useful, and unimportant. They also have time horizons: urgent (to be done as soon as possible), fairly urgent (to be done by a near deadline), not urgent (can wait for a while), and optional (no time pressure). The categories and time horizons determine what you can put at the bottom of the pile, and what must go to the top. Estimate the time each task will take, then plan your days and weeks around achieving the top priority tasks, fitting in the others around them.

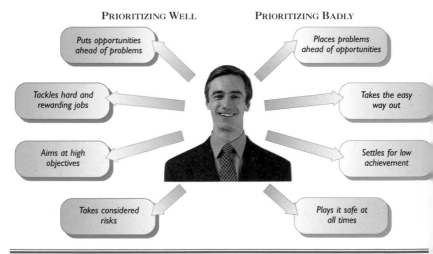

PRIORITIZING WELL

Puts opportunities ahead of problems

Tackles hard and rewarding jobs

Aims at high objectives

Takes considered risks

PRIORITIZING BADLY

Places problems ahead of opportunities

Takes the easy way out

Settles for low achievement

Plays it safe at all times

# DEALING WITH DEADLINES

Avoid the practice of most journalists, whose work is ruled by deadlines, but who usually leave everything until the last minute. When you name or accept a deadline, be sure that the chosen completion date is really necessary. Once a date is agreed, missing the deadline is not acceptable: keeping it becomes a key priority. Work back from the deadline for the main task to see which sub-tasks have to be completed by what time. If possible, build in some room for slippage. You will probably have reason to be grateful for this contingency. If all else fails, though, be prepared to ask for an extension as early as possible. Do not spring any last-minute surprises on anybody.

◀ **AVOIDING A LAST-MINUTE RUSH**
*Set yourself interim deadlines to help you meet a final deadline date. In this way you can work toward achieving your final target in stages, rather than rushing a job at the last minute.*

# PICKING A SPECIALTY

Making the right choices on priorities also applies to improving areas of personal performance. General ability opens the greatest number of doors, but it also pays to give priority to one area in which you can become expert. First, you stand out from the crowd as the person who knows all about the subject. That knowledge could give you a key position in important projects and discussions. Second, the experience of mastering a subject in depth and having total command in your special area bolsters confidence and builds mindpower. Do not choose a specialization that will rarely, if ever, be used. Rather, seek mainstream areas that are vital to the business of the organization, such as organizing market research or setting up new operations.

**65** Make a point of finishing work by the time that you have agreed to.

**66** Do not rely on seniority: rather, win the authority of true expertise.

# UNDERSTANDING MONEY

*The ability to manage money is crucial to any manager. Accounting is not a natural talent for most people, but it is much easier to master than many suppose. The key to becoming a numerate manager is to practice using numbers all the time.*

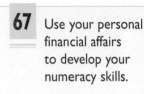

**67** Use your personal financial affairs to develop your numeracy skills.

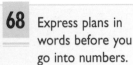

**68** Express plans in words before you go into numbers.

**DEFINING THE KEY ▼ NUMERACY SKILLS**

*This manager has a wide range of aptitudes that make it easier to do his job with full knowledge of the financial consequences and needs.*

## BECOMING NUMERATE

To master basic numeracy skills, you will need to learn from books or in a classroom. Once you understand the principles, there is no substitute for actually drawing up budgets, writing business plans, doing management accounts, and studying financial reports. At first this may be slow and grinding work, but you will become faster and better with experience. Do not let yourself be blinded with science. The simpler, the better is an excellent guide to managing finances.

Uses spreadsheets

Reads balance sheets

Writes business plans

Understands cash flow

Understands management accounts

Optimizes financial returns

# UNDERSTANDING CASH FLOW

You can go bankrupt while still making a profit. The key is cash flow. If bills and wages are paid before customers honor their debts, cash will flow out of the company, possibly in lethal amounts. Effective cash management means speeding the collection of money due, matching your own settlement of accounts to the inward flow, and making good use of the cash balances by investing them for the highest return. When looking at potential profit, always look at the cash flow consequences. Otherwise, you could be crippled by taking on more business than you can finance.

**69** Always have your calculations checked by somebody else.

**70** If you cannot grasp a concept, admit it frankly.

## QUESTIONS TO ASK YOURSELF

**Q** Is there any financial issue I do not follow?

**Q** Am I planning to learn about such matters?

**Q** Can I forecast results with confidence that they will materialize?

**Q** Do I know with fair accuracy how well or poorly my unit will have performed when the period ends?

# LEARNING ACCOUNTING

Every manager should know the principles of double-entry bookkeeping, profit and loss accounts, and balance sheets. But leave applying those principles to professional accountants. As a manager, you are concerned with management accounts, which seek to reflect actual events as closely as possible in financial terms. Training courses will tell you all you need to know about the relationship between income, direct costs, and contribution. You can then concentrate on raising revenue and lowering costs simultaneously – a simple formula, but always effective.

# WRITING AN EFFECTIVE BUSINESS PLAN

Start your plan with a statement that sets down, in words, rather than in numbers, the outcome you hope to achieve. Use a spreadsheet to work out the figures that will result if the targets are met. Be as realistic as possible, and make sure that you tone down any extravagant figures – they will not impress readers. List your assumptions in full, and also note anything that could possibly go wrong. Finally, you should include your reasoned analysis of the cost of losing the opportunity.

# REDUCING STRESS

*S*tress in itself is not harmful, but it can
seriously affect those who react badly
to it. To improve your effectiveness as a
manager, you must be able to recognize your
limits and take action to reduce stress when
it threatens your performance.

**71** Work more effectively, rather than for longer hours.

*Stressed manager is unable to concentrate on task at hand*

## RECOGNIZING THE SIGNS

Everyone reacts to stress differently, but it may
manifest itself in physical symptoms, such as
skin complaints or digestive troubles. You
may feel irritable and run-down. Work
can become obsessive, and nervous
problems can result in depression,
anxiety, or other psychological disorders.
Look out for warning signs and tackle
stress before it becomes debilitating.

◀ **COPING WITH STRESS**
*Deal with stress positively by seeking
support from superiors, close friends, and
colleagues, and priortizing your workload.*

## ANALYZING PERSONALITY

**R**esearch has shown that certain types of people
are more prone to stress and its by-products, such
as heart disease. If you are an ambitious manager
who is extremely competitive, fast in thought,
speech, and action, committed, impatient, and
pressed for time, you are likely to be a Type A
personality – at risk from stress. If you are more
placid, you are less at risk and classed as Type B.
Type A managers may also be tense egotists who
lack self-control and are quick to anger. If you fit
the Type A pattern, modify your behavior to
reduce the chances and incidence of stress.

**72** Discuss personal problems with a wise listener.

**73** Defuse anxieties by listing possible future events, good and bad.

## IDENTIFYING YOUR PERSONALITY TYPE

Read through the following questions. The more "yes" answers you give, the closer you are to the Type A personality. You can reduce your stress levels by adopting the opposite, or Type B, behavior. For example, if you walk and eat rapidly, make a conscious effort to slow down. Do you:

- Feel a constant pressure to get things done?
- Often compete against the clock?
- Always hurry?
- Make decisions quickly?
- Get restless and impatient with being idle?
- Speak fast?
- Always arrive on time?
- Think about and do several things at the same time?
- Move, walk, and eat rapidly?
- Often get impatient?
- See yourself as very ambitious?
- In conversation, display brisk and impatient body movements; taut facial muscles; fist-clenching; explosive and hurried speech patterns; or a lack of bodily relaxation?

## HANDLING ANXIETY

Being anxious is an unpleasant experience. It can have a perfectly understandable cause. A merger or reorganization, for instance, may threaten your job or your powers. Threats produce anxiety. But what action can you take to remove the threat? In the above examples, almost certainly none. However, you should try to calm your anxiety. Avoid listening to rumor and think positively. After all, the threat may not even materialize, in which case, you have made yourself feel awful for nothing. Whatever the cause of the anxiety, identify that cause, develop a plan for removing the cause, if possible, and/or form a contingency plan to cope. Occupying yourself with this three-part formula will lessen anxiety anyway, and could make it wholly unnecessary.

**74** Analyze reasons for procrastination and face them squarely. Then set yourself a deadline for action.

## TACKLING DIFFICULTIES

It is easy to procrastinate, but this habit (which is all but universal) can increase your stress in two ways. First, you may feel guilty about leaving the task undone. Second, you are building up stressful time pressure for the future. Procrastination is itself a symptom of stress. For example, a decision may involve taking a risk, or a necessary action (say, firing somebody) may loom ahead. Your reaction to these stresses may be to delay the evil hour. That is bad stress management. You will still have to grab the bull by the horns, and will pass more stressful hours or days before you do so. Do it now.

# USING STRESS POSITIVELY

A crisis can descend out of the blue, or build up over months. It can affect everyone in an organization, or may be entirely personal, but it is important not to allow yourself to slump into despair. In fact, you can turn the stress of a crisis to your advantage. Because stress raises your levels of adrenaline, you can harness that extra energy to resolve the emergency successfully, if that is feasible. Begin by assessing what can actually be done and whether the crisis can be cured. Then start on a no-holds-barred effort to recover from the disaster. You will benefit from the healthy stress of constructive achievement under pressure.

 **75** Get excited about challenges in a positive manner.

 **76** Find relaxation methods that suit you and use them.

▼ **HANDLING CONFRONTATION**

*In confrontational situations, it is vital to control your own stress levels. The higher those levels rise, the less likely you are to be able to control the discussion. Slow down your breathing, calm down the situation, and concentrate on what you want to achieve.*

*Stressed manager is approached by angry employee*

*Manager controls stress, and resolves disagreement with employee*

*Manager is unable to control stress levels, and situation deteriorates*

# LEARNING TO RELAX

The more effectively you rest, the better you use your energies. Few people, however, make positive use of daytime rests, even though that is one of the best means of controlling stress. Make time during the day to get rid of superfluous and stressful emotions, and to substitute relaxed calm. Many techniques are available, from deep breathing to yoga. What they have in common is mental concentration on non-stressful thoughts, and assertion of self-control over your emotions and body. The most useful techniques are those that can be applied any time and anywhere, such as the relaxation exercise shown right.

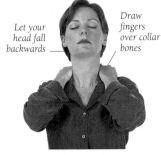

*Let your head fall backwards*

*Draw fingers over collar bones*

## ▲ EASING TENSION

*Place your hands over your shoulders, exhale, let your head fall backwards, and slowly draw your fingers over your collar bones. Repeat several times.*

## RELAXING AT HOME

Relaxation is a technique that can easily be learned. Take time out to enjoy a regular period of relaxation in your busy daily routine. Find a quiet spot in the house, place a rug or mat on the floor, with a cushion, then lie down and begin the exercise.

1. After having a good stretch, sit or lie in a comfortable position, eyes closed.
2. Concentrate your inner attention on a fixed image or point – try the point between and above your eyebrows.
3. Deeply relax your muscles one by one. Start with the feet and work up the legs to the abdomen, chest, shoulders, neck, and face; let your jaw muscles hang loose.
4. Concentrate on your breath passing deeply, easily, and naturally through the

nose, silently repeating the word "one" (or a mantra if you have one) every time you breathe out.
5. Allow yourself to relax completely.
6. If music helps, have it playing softly. Conjure up images of warm climates, and try to imagine your body becoming warmer and heavier.
7. Continue for 10 to 20 minutes; if you fall asleep or doze, it doesn't matter, you are still relaxing.

### RELAXING THE BODY ▶
*Lie in a comfortable position, supporting your head with a cushion or pillow, and relax your entire body.*

*Breathe through nose*

*Relax from feet upward*

# ASSESSING PROGRESS

*Frequent and accurate assessment of progress is essential to improving effectiveness. That requires facts, and managers must find ways to measure their standards effectively in order to set new targets for performing even better in future.*

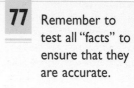

**77** Remember to test all "facts" to ensure that they are accurate.

## SEEKING FACTS

How will you know if you have succeeded in a particular activity? Feeling good is pleasant but inadequate. It is far better to target an activity in a meaningful way by applying total quality management principles to your work. This means finding key activities where you can set and measure your standards. For example, an item on your list could be arriving at meetings on time, for which you set a standard of 100 percent. By setting factual targets, you give yourself defined objectives whose achievement nobody can dispute. Tell colleagues about your aims so that they can point out whenever you fail to perform to standard.

▲ **MEASURING YOUR STANDARDS**
*Factual targets help you to gauge your performance. For example, if you set yourself a target of answering the telephone within five rings, you are setting a standard that is easily measured.*

**78** If you set high standards for yourself, be sure to keep to them.

## DO'S AND DON'TS

✔ Do be a hard judge of yourself.

✔ Do have a good idea of what you want to achieve and why.

✔ Do share the credit for achievement.

✔ Do admit failings.

✘ Don't congratulate yourself on what other people did.

✘ Don't get carried away by success.

✘ Don't be boastful.

✘ Don't be misled by past comparisons.

# ANALYZING SUCCESS

Success can be your enemy. If you have enjoyed a period of great prosperity and are well ahead of your competitors, the temptation is to count the money, lie back, and rest on your laurels. That is the moment when slackness begins to creep in. It is important to analyze success as carefully as failure. What special circumstances, outside your control, contributed to the excellent results? After allowing for these, how well did you really do? What could have been done better, with still better results? Most important, what are you going to do for an encore? The objective is to make success a platform for further advance. What matters most is the new target, not the past.

## REVIEWING YOUR PERFORMANCE

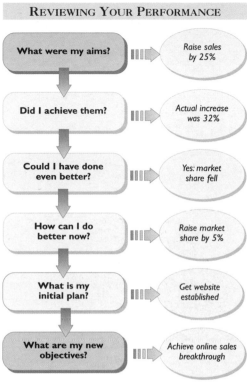

| What were my aims? | Raise sales by 25% |
| Did I achieve them? | Actual increase was 32% |
| Could I have done even better? | Yes: market share fell |
| How can I do better now? | Raise market share by 5% |
| What is my initial plan? | Get website established |
| What are my new objectives? | Achieve online sales breakthrough |

# USING COMPARISONS

Comparing one set of results with another is the basis of management accounting. But such comparisons can be misleading. If sales growth slumps from 20 percent to 5 percent, then rises again to 15 percent, that figure is triple the previous year's outcome, but still a quarter below the achievement two years ago. Before hailing today's figures, check that the basis for comparison neither exaggerates nor depreciates your success. For accuracy, compare the past 12 months against the preceding 12 at the end of each quarter.

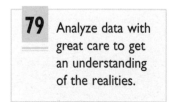

**79** Analyze data with great care to get an understanding of the realities.

# ACHIEVING SUCCESS

Success hinges on the ability to manage your career well. Take every opportunity to advance yourself, and enlist help from others to further your progress.

## REASSESSING YOUR GOALS

*Dispassionate and methodical analysis of goals is essential to the success of your vision. But situations can change. You must be prepared constantly to reassess and adapt your ideas as necessary. Use this assessment process to find ways to take decisive action.*

**80** Probe deeply into questions to get answers – obvious ones can be wrong.

**81** Take objections seriously until proven mistaken.

**82** Train everybody in sound methods of investigation.

### ASKING QUESTIONS

When assessing future goals, always analyze them carefully. Never take anything for granted. In other words, always ask questions until you are satisfied that, as far as possible, you know the whole truth. The vital word in your vocabulary is "Why?". Then you need other short words: "What?", "How?", "Who?", and "When?". The analytical "Why?" questions lead on to: What can be done? How can that be achieved? Who will carry out the implementation? When will the action be taken? At all stages, further questions will arise. Do not leave the answers dangling in the air.

# USING THE ANSWERS

The phrase "paralysis by analysis" refers to organizations that spend months on number-crunching and reports and then do nothing. Once you have decided on your goals, if you find it difficult to take action, ask yourself why. Perhaps the effort required is itself inhibiting. Or you may be concerned that once you have moved, it will be hard, maybe impossible, to turn back. So the fear of being wrong, with awful consequences, can paralyze you. By all means try for a "fail-safe" position, so that, if the worst comes to the worst, the situation will be tolerable. But if you have obtained the answers on the "What?" and "How?", make sure you act on them to pursue your goals.

**83** Be biased in favor of taking action as soon as possible.

**84** Set a time limit on discussion, but be flexible if it proves inadequate.

## TAKING ACTION

On taking action to reach your goals, you have two options. One is to follow your chosen path regardless of events. The other is to observe all the outcomes, and to adapt your plan, radically if need be, to improve the chances of success. The first course sometimes works, but equally can lead to disaster. The second course contains the risk that, by pulling back in the face of adversity, you will miss the initial objective when it could have been reached. The correct approach uses elements of both options. Provided the objective still makes sense, concentrate your drive on reaching that goal.

*Manager revises goal after hearing comments*

*Team member supports colleague's view*

*Colleague makes an important point*

**CHANGING COURSE ▶**
*Listen to the opinions of associates. You may learn something that will prompt you to adapt your actions and improve the chances of success.*

# FINDING MENTORS

*E*verybody can think of other people who
have had a profound influence on their
life and work. Learning from mentors, whose
experience is more varied and greater than
your own, is a key to improving your
performance and achieving success.

**85** Keep in touch with
people who have
previously advised
you well.

## LEARNING FROM OTHERS

**A** mentor may be a parent, teacher, university
lecturer, boss, or close friend. The principle is
always the same. Your performance is improved
by listening to and learning from knowledgeable
minds. You can choose mentors from the past,
and indeed many successful businessmen have
borrowed ideas from dead business heroes.
However, bygone inspirations are no substitute for
living advisers, who can listen to your problems
and hopes and react as circumstances demand.

**86** Learn from
books on and by
great managers.

**ASSESSING A ▼
MENTOR'S QUALITIES**
*There are several important qualities you
should look for in a mentor. He or she will
be listening to your problems and hopes
and reacting to them, so trust is vital.*

Possesses high integrity,
honesty, and credibility

Insists on getting
things done

Insists on the
highest standards

Demonstrates the ability
to envisage the future

Sets an
inspirational
example

Shows deep
concern for others'
performance

# FINDING ALLIES

Selecting the right mentor is an important step toward optimizing your performance. He or she does not necessarily have to be an equal or a superior. They could be a key subordinate, or a colleague of different status. The vital role is to provide talents and resources that you lack. In a career, you may have many different mentors; or one may be at your side for the whole journey, or most of it. Always look for a suitable ally you feel you can work with closely, and whose judgment you will respect.

*Mentor rejects ideas out of hand*

*Partner distrusts mentor's opinion*

**POOR CHOICE**

*Mentor gives dispassionate advice*

*Partner respects mentor's views*

**GOOD CHOICE**

**CHOOSING A MENTOR ▶**
*You need to work closely with someone who knows you and your weaknesses well and on whom you can rely for dispassionate advice.*

## USING THE BOSS

A good boss is an excellent mentor, whose example and teaching can guide you for a whole career. Even an able leader who spares no time for deliberate coaching can provide information and inspiration. Watch what these exemplars do, and borrow what seems to work best. Much of what they teach will have to do with style and instinct, but these imponderables can make all the difference. Use the boss not only as a source of "lessons and war stories" (which other senior people can also provide), but as a sounding board for your own ideas and ambitions.

**87** Look out for the partner who adds to your powers.

**88** Do not be shy about approaching others for help in managing.

# MAKING CONTACTS

*It is not only what you know, but who you know that often makes the difference between success and failure. Your address book is one of the most valuable tools in your possession, and one that will improve greatly in value over time.*

**89** Make an effort to meet friends working in other companies.

**90** Meet frequently with contacts for non-business talks.

**91** Back up face-to-face contacts with the telephone and email.

## KEEPING A RECORD

Effective careerists write down the names of every useful or potentially useful contact they make, and periodically update the names, addresses, and contact numbers. It does not matter whether you keep the list in a book or a computer program, although updating and back-up are much easier with the latter. Back-up is important, since losing an uncopied organizer or address book can have disastrous consequences. Cross-reference names, businesses, and areas of expertise wherever possible.

## REMEMBERING CONTACTS

A contact whom you forget has lost his or her value. Try to memorize a new contact's name. Get all their details and put these facts on the record (computer programs are ideal). Take every contact seriously. You never know when or in what valuable context you may meet people again.

*Manager meets new contact and exchanges business cards*

▲ **MEETING NEW CONTACTS**
*When you meet somebody, use their name as often as possible in the conversation to help you remember it. Get a business card, and ask about their job and where they live. A new contact may have skills or contacts that will assist you or your colleagues.*

## STAYING IN TOUCH

Some of your best contacts will be made at work, especially when working in teams. Teams can operate inside departments, or across both departments and functions, and may well involve others outside the company. You can learn much from fellow members, whether as a team member or leader. At close quarters, you learn the strengths and weaknesses of fellow members. To make the relationship successful and lasting, put the team's collective success before your own. To earn their respect, ask for other people's opinion of your contribution, and act on their constructive criticism. Do not be afraid to speak out yourself. Finally, be frank with criticism, but generous with praise, and keep in touch with the colleagues you value.

**92** Try to help when contacts ask you for assistance.

*Colleague returns favor by helping manager out of a difficult situation*

*Manager recommends contact to a colleague who is looking for help*

**93** Treat the team as a band of closely knit colleagues, and keep up the relationship later on.

### KEEPING THE ► TEAM TOGETHER

*Charles knew that, collectively, his team possessed many strengths, and that there was still a great deal that could be achieved together. Using business contacts he had made in the industry, he was able to lead their move en masse to a new employer. This benefited the team as a whole, helped the new employer, and enhanced Charles' reputation as a successful team leader.*

**CASE STUDY**
Charles had the good fortune early in his career to take charge of a team of bright young managers who formed a highly skilled staff group, specializing in statistical analysis of tough problems. A change in management meant that the team's future was uncertain. The members were ready to set about finding futures independently. But Charles realized that he was unlikely ever to find such

an exceptional group again. He persuaded his colleagues to sell themselves as one package to one employer. The most promising choice was a major manufacturer that was in deep trouble. Charles led the team over to this second employer, where they helped in a big turnaround. Charles and two team colleagues then left to start their own firm in another, rising industry. They made a large fortune.

# TAKING THE LEAD

*The more you can show and exercise the attributes of leadership, the more likely you are to succeed. Take the initiative and seek out every opportunity to develop your leadership skills. Your experience will stand you in good stead for the future.*

**94** Choose the moment to lead, and then be decisive.

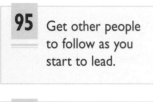

**95** Get other people to follow as you start to lead.

**96** Turn down a role unless you have the means to master it properly.

## SEEKING OPPORTUNITIES

You do not have to wait for an appointment to a leadership position to lead. The chances are that you will be involved in a task force or similar group, or you may be singled out for a particular project. Either event provides an opportunity to push yourself forward by proposing a new idea or by taking up a strong position and becoming its powerful advocate. Be prepared to implement what you have proposed.

▼ **TAKING THE INITIATIVE**
*Get into the habit of volunteering to lead or take on extra responsibility – you will gain invaluable experience. He, or she, who hesitates, or shows no interest, will gain nothing.*

*Manager askes for volunteer to run project*

*Eager colleague is quick to volunteer*

*Collegue shows interest but hesitates*

*Employee is bored and disinterested*

# SPEAKING OUT

If you have a good idea, have the courage of your convictions, and use your conviction to carry the plan through to acceptance, completion, and success. Reluctance to "stick my neck out" holds back careers – and organizations. The worst you can experience is a refusal. For the best chance of success, be prudent in choosing when to make proposals, and be careful to test them by analysis or by asking close and trusted colleagues.

**97** Avoid changing your opinions to match those of the majority.

## FINDING ROLES TO BUILD LEADERSHIP SKILLS

| WAYS TO LEAD | SKILLS TO BE GAINED |
| --- | --- |
| JOIN A TASK FORCE<br>These are usually formed to tackle specific issues. | ● Provides excellent experience in directing teams and meeting deadlines.<br>● Involves start-to-finish identification with task. |
| JOIN A PROJECT TEAM<br>These bring multi-skilled individuals together to accomplish major plans. | ● Usually provides exposure to other disciplines and functions.<br>● Develops a wider range of personal abilities. |
| APPLY FOR PROMOTION<br>An appointment to a higher post may involve leading others. | ● Offers the chance to bring fresh vision to a job.<br>● Provides the opportunity to understand a new role and experience processes from a different perspective. |
| PROPOSE CHANGE<br>Suggest ways of making individual and team improvements. | ● Any change initiative brings chances of proposing and leading specific projects.<br>● Engages initiative and powers of persuasion. |
| LEAD A SUB-UNIT<br>Take on responsibility for delivering personal profits. | ● Brings challenge of meeting self-set targets.<br>● Given adequate scope, allows leadership to be shown in a highly visible way. |
| RESOLVE A CRISIS SITUATION<br>Take a lead in any demanding emergency action. | ● Pressure of necessity removes barriers to asserting personal authority.<br>● Encourages capacity for fast, decisive action. |

# INFLUENCING OTHERS

*Convincing others to accept your point of view, ideas, and action plans is essential to success. In debates, negotiations, and confrontations, you cannot expect your view to prevail every time. But you can usually work toward an acceptable compromise.*

**98** Put your position over clearly, but keep in mind that of the other party.

## CULTURAL DIFFERENCES

Japanese negotiators may come in a large team and retire for group discussions before giving their response. Americans like to have lawyers present and are very concerned with contractual obligations. Germans value business relationships highly and expect the other side to show equal respect for promises given.

## CONVINCING PEOPLE

The first requisite in any debate is to convince yourself. Have a closely reasoned, fact-based case that you have thoroughly examined. Second, while emotions such as enthusiasm are highly desirable in argument, do not allow yourself to become emotional in the sense of losing control. You need control to guide the debate toward the end you want. If others become overly emotional, try to calm the discussion. Never lose sight of your objective, but be prepared to concede some points where facts or diplomacy demand. Above all, seek to persuade the others that your decision or choice is also theirs.

## NEGOTIATING TO WIN

Always go into negotiations with a clear idea of the highest outcome you want, what you expect will result, and the lowest acceptable result. You may find that all three ideas change during the course of talks, especially if they are protracted. It helps if you can get the other side to name their proposals first. Then you have a straightforward choice between accepting or asking for more. If you have to play your cards first, do not tone down your proposition to what you think the other side will accept. Never say "no" for somebody else. They will say it themselves soon enough.

### POINTS TO REMEMBER

- You should be prepared to change your tactics in order to win agreement.
- The other side should be regarded as partners and not as enemies to be defeated.
- Avoid saying or doing anything rash – you may want to deal with the other side again.
- Keep something in reserve that can be placed on the table should the necessity arise.

## DEALING WITH DIFFERENT TYPES OF NEGOTIATION

| TYPE OF NEGOTIATION | HANDLING METHODS |
| --- | --- |
| **RESOLVING DISPUTES** Meeting to troubleshoot. | ● Seek to obtain the trust of both sides to the dispute. ● Start by establishing an agreed description of the facts. ● Do not allow proceedings to become heated or abusive. |
| **BECOMING PARTNERS** Setting up a working relationship. | ● Cover essential items clearly in any exchange of letters. ● Resort to full legal agreements only if you have to. ● Allow escape clauses for either side on fair terms. |
| **AGREEING CONTRACTS** Formalizing commercial relationships. | ● Avoid loading the other side with demanding commitments. ● Watch out carefully for unintended or intended traps. ● Make sure both sides are negotiating in good faith. |
| **SETTLING PRICES** Making one-time deals, not installed payment. | ● If you are in the stronger position, do not abuse it. ● Try to establish the highest price the deal will bear. ● Leave room for both sides to make adequate profits. |
| **INDIVIDUAL PACKAGES** Discussing an employee's rewards. | ● Prepare your preferred package before the meeting. ● Expect comparisons with other employees and organizations. ● Be prepared to listen to reasonable demands. |
| **COLLECTIVE BARGAINING** Meeting workers' representatives to discuss pay and other issues. | ● Cut through inherent animosity or distrust. ● Be firm but sympathetic and willing to compromise. ● Remember that workers rarely strike on non-pay issues. |

**99** Call a recess if discussions become overheated and tempers rise.

## ACCEPTING COMPROMISE

If two propositions are far apart, look for other areas where you can readily agree, and either reach that agreement before returning to the main subject or save it for use as a bargaining counter. Resist the temptation to "defeat" the other side. The best outcome is when both sides are fully satisfied that the result is both in their best interests and the best they could have achieved. Try for that.

# PLANNING AHEAD

*People who plan their careers mostly outperform those who leave their progress to chance. The plan will probably include changing employers, which has become highly acceptable, as has breaking away to develop an independent career.*

**100** Plan to achieve more than you expect – you may well get there.

## LOOKING TO THE FUTURE

Results for individuals, as for companies, are almost invariably improved by thinking ahead. The natural planning period is the year. By working out a detailed 12-month program and putting it down on paper, you effectively concentrate the mind on what you want to achieve. You also provide yourself with a touchstone for your subsequent decisions. Will they advance you toward these annual goals? If not, you should think again.

This Year's Goals
- Master colloquial French
- Achieve promotion to job with profit responsibility
- Prepare ground for future role inside Single Market
- Join a key corporate task force
- Form club of ambitious young executives
- Become expert in use of ecommerce

◀ **LISTING YOUR GOALS**
*An excellent habit is to write down, each year, what goals you want to achieve over the next 12 months. This exercise forces you to think about your real aims and possibilities.*

## CHANGING JOBS

The most important steps in your progress will almost certainly involve changing jobs, probably companies, and possibly countries. Job-hopping was once a potential liability, but may now even be an asset. Changes usually involve extra money and other benefits. While this matters very much, never make it the only reason for changing. The interest and challenge of the job itself are paramount. If you are changing organizations, research carefully the nature and prospects of the new employer before you make your move.

**101** If you miss a career target, name a new one and start again.

# AIMING FOR THE TOP

The summit of a management career is reaching the rank of chief executive of a major company. Obviously, only a minority ever reach the peak, but ambitious executives expect to be among those few and prepare themselves accordingly. A career presents other opportunities of taking charge and showing that you are capable of controlling and directing an operation toward your chosen goal. Above all, you need people skills. Practice getting people to work with you and for you productively throughout your ascent. Harness those skills to confidence and vision – a clear sense of the future you want to achieve – and you have a good chance of scaling the summit.

## QUESTIONS TO ASK YOURSELF

Q Is it time for me to start thinking of a new career move?

Q What is the ideal position to provide greater experience and challenge?

Q Realistically, is there any reason why I cannot reach the top?

Q Can I do anything to remove the blockage and rise higher?

Q Where do I want to be at intervals of five years from now?

Q What must be done to reach those destinations?

## BECOMING INDEPENDENT

Sometimes leaving the corporate world for independent work is forced through redundancy. Those organizations that downsize or become virtual may well "outsource" activities, often employing former executives and experts as freelancers. In other cases, people resign to exploit business opportunities, sometimes ones they have spotted during their employment. It is advisable to keep the possibility of breaking away in mind, so long as you recognize that the skills needed for independent success are quite different, and that life is likely to be less comfortable, more solitary, and more uncertain outside the security of the corporate fold.

**▲ SETTING UP ON YOUR OWN**
*Being your own boss can be challenging and exciting. With the advent of email and the Internet, many more people are now taking the opportunity to work from home.*

# ASSESSING YOUR ABILITY

Working towards excellence presents a lifelong challenge and opportunity. The following questionnaire will help you to evaluate your strengths and weaknesses and decide where to place the most effort to achieve still more. If your answer is "never", mark Option 1; if it is "always", mark Option 4; and so on. Add your scores together, and refer to the Analysis to see how you scored. Answering as honestly as you can is a good start towards self-improvement.

| OPTIONS |
| --- |
| 1 Never |
| 2 Occasionally |
| 3 Frequently |
| 4 Always |

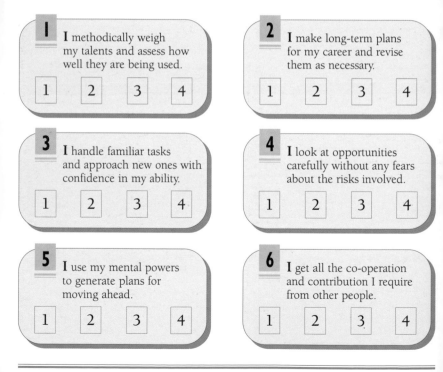

**1** I methodically weigh my talents and assess how well they are being used.

1   2   3   4

**2** I make long-term plans for my career and revise them as necessary.

1   2   3   4

**3** I handle familiar tasks and approach new ones with confidence in my ability.

1   2   3   4

**4** I look at opportunities carefully without any fears about the risks involved.

1   2   3   4

**5** I use my mental powers to generate plans for moving ahead.

1   2   3   4

**6** I get all the co-operation and contribution I require from other people.

1   2   3   4

**7** I exercise to maintain fitness standards and keep close to my ideal weight.

1   2   3   4

**8** I eat and sleep well and am careful to avoid working excessive hours.

1   2   3   4

**9** I aim to achieve excellence, and work on areas where I fall short.

1   2   3   4

**10** I strive to win by outdoing the competition on every important aspect.

1   2   3   4

**11** I set aside time to master new and useful training and education.

1   2   3   4

**12** I apply organized mental techniques to help me think more effectively.

1   2   3   4

**13** I recall everything I need to remember readily and without difficulty.

1   2   3   4

**14** I work to improve my reading speed without loss of comprehension.

1   2   3   4

**15** I seek feedback about my writing and speaking, and act on any criticisms.

1   2   3   4

**16** I enjoy giving talks and welcome opportunities to appear before an audience.

1   2   3   4

**17** I look for new ideas from others and seek to develop new ideas myself.

| 1 | 2 | 3 | 4 |

**18** I systematically manage my time and act to eliminate any waste.

| 1 | 2 | 3 | 4 |

**19** I have, and apply, meaningful measures of my personal productivity.

| 1 | 2 | 3 | 4 |

**20** I compile a list of priorities and organize my work accordingly.

| 1 | 2 | 3 | 4 |

**21** I apply competent numeracy and financial know-how to my activities.

| 1 | 2 | 3 | 4 |

**22** I act to cope with negative states like anxiety, guilt, and undue stress.

| 1 | 2 | 3 | 4 |

**23** I find ways of achieving relaxation and I use those methods effectively.

| 1 | 2 | 3 | 4 |

**24** I regard success as the stepping-stone to further, greater achievement.

| 1 | 2 | 3 | 4 |

**25** I take care to analyze issues thoroughly, but I also act decisively.

| 1 | 2 | 3 | 4 |

**26** I turn to valued advisers to help me with personal and business issues.

| 1 | 2 | 3 | 4 |

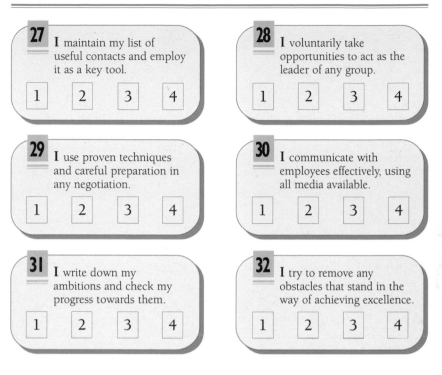

**27** I maintain my list of useful contacts and employ it as a key tool.

1 | 2 | 3 | 4

**28** I voluntarily take opportunities to act as the leader of any group.

1 | 2 | 3 | 4

**29** I use proven techniques and careful preparation in any negotiation.

1 | 2 | 3 | 4

**30** I communicate with employees effectively, using all media available.

1 | 2 | 3 | 4

**31** I write down my ambitions and check my progress towards them.

1 | 2 | 3 | 4

**32** I try to remove any obstacles that stand in the way of achieving excellence.

1 | 2 | 3 | 4

## ANALYSIS

Now you have completed the self-assessment, add up the scores and check your performance by referring to the corresponding evaluations:

**32–63:** You are falling far short of achieving excellence. Forget the excuses and face up to the realities of your working life. You can do better. The only thing that is missing is the will to act. Find that will, and improvement will come.

**64–95:** You have advanced a fair way toward using your powers to the full. Now take stock, using the questionnaire, to choose the areas where you can most valuably boost your achievement. The payoff should be very quick.

**96–128:** You have a full and highly effective working life. But you can still achieve much more. You know that, which is one reason why you are doing so well. Keep it up.

# INDEX

# ACKNOWLEDGMENTS

## AUTHOR'S ACKNOWLEDGMENTS

This book owes its existence to the perceptive inspiration of Stephanie Jackson and Nigel Duffield at Dorling Kindersley; and I owe more than I can say to the expertise and enthusiasm of Jane Simmonds and all the editorial and design staff who worked on the project. I am also greatly indebted to the many colleagues, friends, and other management luminaries on whose wisdom and information I have drawn.

## PUBLISHER'S ACKNOWLEDGMENTS

Dorling Kindersley would like to thank the following for their help and participation in producing this book:

**Editorial** Alison Bolus, Michael Downey, Nicola Munro, Jane Simmonds, David Tombesi-Walton, Sylvia Tombesi-Walton; **Indexer** Hilary Bird.

**Design** Pauline Clarke, Jamie Hanson, Nigel Morris, Tish Mills.

**DTP assistance** Rob Campbell.

**Photography** Steve Gorton; **Photography assistance** Nici Harper, Andy Komorowski.

**Models** Phil Argent, Carol Evans, John Gillard, Richard Hill, Cornell John, Janey Madlani, Karen Murray, Mutsumi Niwa, Suki Tan, Peter Taylor, Wendy Yun.

**Makeup** Debbie Finlow, Janice Tee.

**Suppliers** Austin Reed, Bally, Church & Co., Clark Davis & Co. Ltd, Compaq, David Clulow Opticians, Elonex, Escada, Filofax, Gateway 2000, Geiger Brickel, Jones Bootmakers, Moss Bros, Mucci Bags, Staverton. With thanks to Tony Ash at Geiger Brickel (Office Furniture) and Carron Williams at Bally (Shoes).

**Picture research** Andy Sansom; **Picture library assistance** Sue Hadley, Rachel Hilford, Denise O'Brien, Melanie Simmonds.

## PICTURE CREDITS

Key: *a* above, *b* bottom, *c* centre, *l* left, *r* right, *t* top
**Allsport** John Cameron/APL/AllsportUSA 14; **Powerstock/ZEFA** 18, 21, John Lawrence 37; **Telegraph Colour Library** B&M Productions 24; **Tony Stone Images** Bruce Ayres 41, John Blaustein 65, Donovan Reese 4, front jacket *tl*; **Elizabeth Whiting Associates** 12.

---

## AUTHOR'S BIOGRAPHY

Robert Heller is a leading authority in the world of management consulting and was the founding editor of Britain's top management magazine, *Management Today*. He is much in demand as a conference speaker in Europe, North and South America, and the Far East. As editorial director of Haymarket Publishing Group, Robert Heller supervised the launch of several highly successful magazines such as *Campaign*, *Computing*, and *Accountancy Age*. His many acclaimed – and worldwide best-selling – books include *The Naked Manager*, *Culture Shock*, *The Age of the Common Millionaire*, *The Way to Win* (with Will Carling), *The Complete Guide to Modern Management*, and *In Search of European Excellence*. Robert Heller has also written a number of earlier books in the Dorling Kindersley *Essential Managers* series.